Notes from a Nappy-Headed Poet

Vol. 1:

Song for Mama

Valerie Elaine Deering

MANIFOLD GRACE
Publishing House LLC

Notes from a Nappy Headed Poet Vol. 1: Song for Mama

Cover design: Creativelogoart

ISBN: 978-1-952926-02-0

Printed in the United States of America

Published by Manifold Grace Publishing House, LLC
www.manifoldgracepublishinghouse.com
Southfield, Michigan 48033

Dedication

A song for Mama

A song for my mama

and the gift of her life,

A song for my mama

cause her song

saw us through

A song for my mama

cause she paid her dues!

With Grace and Mercy as her guide

That love song she sang

made us thrive!

Me, sisters, brother, daddy too

My dear Mama

My song for you!

Acknowledgments

Without Great Omniscient Divinity (G.O.D.), my being and this work is impossible. For these gifts I shout Hallelujah! For Divine inspiration, I am eternally grateful!

I stand on shoulders of love, support and kindness, blessed by a sweet elixir of grace and mercy. It would take a book to list them all! That being said, I would like to acknowledge the following blessings:

William and Elizabeth Bryant, Rosalie and Solomon Deering, whose roots anchor the tree from which I sprang;

William and Evelyne Bryant Deering; nurtured and fortified those roots;

The Deering Girls, sisters: Rosemary, Karyne, Jennifer and Myra Jo, brother Billy. My sister from another mother, Abrilla Robinson. They have always had my back through good, bad, and mad, showing me the beauty in Family.

Belinda Bell, beloved spouse, who has loved, supported me and managed to somehow stop the insanity and remember we are better together;

Her beloved mother, Protee who loved me as her own.

Aunts, uncles, cousins near and far, nieces, nephews too, adding spice to a remarkable stew;

My 'Back in the Day' gang from Longfellow Elementary that still accompanies me on this journey;

My Cass Tech classmates, still providing inspiration and thought-provoking conversation that stimulates a beloved community;

My Marygrove Angels, in so many significant ways a wind beneath my wings;

Friends, family from Detroit, Chicago, California, Birmingham, Al., those near and far. Thank you for all you are!

Thank you Ron!

Contents

FOREWORD

We were seventeen when we both walked onto the steps of Marygrove College. From that moment, and throughout our college journey, Val Deering was a presence, a force, a voice. When she entered the room, she owned it. Her passion, shared through her written and verbal power, drew people to her. She met them in their own space with honesty, anger, promise and redemption.

Val's words have taken colleagues, friends and family members through decades of personal, social and political pain, opportunity, rebirth and trauma. Her words have spoken to our hearts, minds and souls in midnight dorm rooms, impromptu luncheons, college reunions, weddings, funerals and many other private moments.

This collection of Val's authentic, powerful, insightful, humane words will energize you, engage you and challenge you. They will make you think, make you feel, make you hurt and help you heal.

Val Deering will speak to you, through you and for you.

Kathleen Alessandro

ꟿNTRO

My mother blessed me with a thirst for knowledge and a love of the written and spoken word. At an early age I began writing plays that I made my sisters and cousins perform, in the basement of our family home. The playwriting later evolved to writing poetry, a joy I have been at for most of my life.

My mother encouraged and supported me in this endeavor and would often ask me to write a poem for special family occasions, particularly about the lives of family members. Knowing our family history and getting a sense of the spirit of a person mattered greatly to her. She wanted us to have footprints in time that celebrated and honored our being and could serve as inspiration and hope for future generations.

Mama was black, proud, and conversant in all things cultural. The Deering House rocked! Books, magazines: Jet and Ebony, The Michigan Chronicle and the newspaper every day! You better READ! And, oh my! The music, the music! It filled our home with warmth and spirit. From classical, gospel, rhythm and blues, jazz, Motown ... Mama was up on it! There wasn't too much that escaped her attention. Friends and family often stopped by to converse and recreate with Mama.

This book is comprised of poems written over time and spaces and different places. For my people, my mama... This book was written from hope and dreams

I pray you laugh
and dance, sing!
From love, for love
This book was written
From my soul
For My people
Mama!
Enjoy!

We are a Family

We Are
A Family
We may argue and disagree

But
We will not be
Disagreeable

We Are
A Family
Each
Seeking
To express
Divinity

We Are
A Family
Hoping, coping
Slipping, gripping
Mindful of
Forgiving

We Are
A Family
Mindful, careful
Constant
Prayerful

QUILTS

Quilts ...
Composed of
Seemingly random
Pieces
haphazardly stitched
together
forming
a whole covering
Pieces of schemes...
Realized dreams ...
Tattered
Some discarded...
Pieces...
That form
<u>All</u>
Of a whole
Quilt
That says:
Me!

BEAUTY SHOP

Beauty Shop
is the place
from way back when
Where sista girls go

To regain their wind!
From the basements and kitchens
Glamour halls and shops
From days of Cleopatra
To what's happenin'
Now!
We go Beauty Shop
Get our WOW!!!
Hair to nails
Face and feet
We go Beauty Shop
Reload and recharge!!
Talk a little trash
While we be getting'
Sweet
We go Beauty Shop
Sweet retreat!
Haircuts and filings
Colorings and plucks
We go Beauty Shop
Pick Spirit Up!!
So be blue
Simmerin' in a nasty, funky stew•..
Go visit Beauty Shop
Find Pretty You!!

The Tenement

Corralled
in concrete towers
Like concrete cells
Not heaven on earth
A particular kind of hell
Where kindness is sublime
Lives bought for nickels and dimes
Quagmires of crime
People bide their time
Where Life is defined
By the desperation of time
And longing...
And
The rhythm in the walk
The jive in the talk
The hope in a dream
Giving the eye a gleam
Blooming in the tenement
Where kindness is sublime
As we struggle
To hold the line...

SHOWINGS

Take me to your house!
Show me where you live!
Lead me to your heart...
I'll lead you to mine!
Undressing my soul
For just your eyes...
Oh...
So Divine!!

Kiss me where I ache
Feel me where I'm wet...
I'm sharing my house
We aren't done yet!

Show me your gardens
With exotic flowers in bloom
I'll shine my sun
In all your varied rooms!

Show me your you
The one I must
Close
My eyes
To see...

You and me together...
What Sublimity!

Nigga

Nigga, nigga
Yo' mama
Yo' daddy
All you nappy headed
kids
Playin' in alleys
Thinkin' its cool to be
Actin' like a word
That's meant
death
For you and me
Lynching, castration
Rape and mutilation...
That's what the word
Nigga
Means to me!
Nigga, nigga
Can't go there

'Cause nigga is a word
Steeped
With despair!
Nigga, nigga
Word bandied about
Like it's the ultimate
Good Spirit SHOUT
People, people
Can't you feel
The spirit of a nigga
Is filled
With ill will!
Nigga, nigga
Don't you know
If there is
HELL
That's where niggas
go!

Notes from a Nappy Headed Sister

Talk about my nappy head
Its kinks and its curls
But once this nappy head
Helped to rule a world!

Today this nappy head
Sometimes bows in defeat
Weeping tears of
Bloody, murderous rage
Centuries deep!

Crying for our children
Lost and alone...
Praying for our children
To find a way
Home!

The road Home is not so difficult to find
If we just use these nappy heads
To guide us to Divine...

For the children,
Need the children,
Teach the children,
Love all of the babies!

DRUNK ON THE WINE OF THE WORLD

Drunk on the wine of the world
Ditty boppin', skirt poppin'
Twirl,
Twirl, Twirl
Drunk on the wine of the world

Club hoppin'
Flip-floppin'
Bling, bling, bling
Drunk...

Life is a trip
When we be too flip
Getting' drunk
On the
Wine of the world!

TELLING TIME BY A TREE

Green
Turn brown
Fall
down
Barren
Bud
Green

FALL

Fall
Falls
Down
All around
Red ... yellow ... brown
Pretty leaves
On the ground

Youth

Youth is:
Angles and lines
This or that
Yes or no
Now or never
And yes
We live forever!

CONVICTED

Descendants of the people
who believed
practiced
slavery

Still stand
In front of the
Schoolhouse door
Lips drippin'
Words:
Nullification
Justadegration

Convicted by deeds
planted in some seeds
these people
descendants
of those
who believed
practiced
slavery
Still stand
In front of the
Schoolhouse door!

ℬEND

Bend, don't break
Flexibility is essential
For only by bending
Is life made simple

Cultivate culture
Embrace the arts
Experiencing culture
Sets you apart

Well rounded, whole
Renaissance wise
A woman forever
Able to rise

Spirit exalted
United and free
Joined with God
in Divine harmony!

The Rent Party

Nickels, quarters, dimes
Gather the coins
Don't be last in line
Coming together to save our kind
From the streets
Lined up at the door
All colors, stripes
And hues
So our people
Wouldn't have the blues
In the street.
Fried chicken, fish, hot sausage too
Sizzlin' in the pan
With the funky blues!
Light and love
We couldn't lose!
Yeah, that rent party!
Sam, Dinah, and Ray
Puttin' down the beats
Made the people sway!
United in purpose
Bonded by hue
The rent party showed us

What together can do.
Politics, music
The talk of the night
The rent party helped us
To walk in light!
Yeah, the rent party!
Everyday folks
In the movement
At
The rent party!
At the rent party
Who knew who you might see
The people were the stars
Walking free!
The rent party
Where together we made a way
For the home folk to gather
And
Save the day!

BITCHES

While
You be
Bitchin'
Uswimmen
You be Dissin'
Some of us
Join in too
More disrespect
Somethin'
I never did expect!

BUT
The most important point
You be missin'
Yo' mamas
Sisters, daughters
Aunties too
Those who lay
Down
To deliver you
Tell me
'Cause they
Wimmen
Ain't they
Bitches
Too...

ℐ GOT MY SEXY BACK

I got my sexy back!
My swerve and curve
Gone wreck your nerve!

I got my sexy back!

Thought it was gone
Time had moved on
BUT
The truth is
It never left
Just got buried
In some mess

I got my sexy back!

Stress and pain
Made me plain
Bills, ills
Material world,
Material girl
Filled me with fright

Stepped out of the light!
Stole my pride

Had me in a dither
Tried to make me
wither
But the God I serve
Is a God of nerve
Seeing me through
The ups and downs
Around and around

Swerve! Curve!

Give God your heart
And all of your mind
A miracle is worked
every time!

So, when you think
Your sexy is gone
Look to God
He'll turn you on!!!

I got my sexy back!!

Some

Need some...
Want some..
Sure could use
Some...

Chantin' for some
Weepin' for some
Holdin' out
For just the right
some... Prayin' for
some
Waitin' for some
Even
Hurtin' for some

Your breath
That softsilkybreeze
Caressin' my body
Makin' me
moan
for some

Lookin' for some
Speakin' for some
Called your name
Socializin' for some

Runnin' for some
Socializin' for some
Waitin' for some
Doin' what a sista does
Tryin' to get her some!

Nails polished for some
Lips painted for some

Body perfumed for some
Dressed in silks and lace
Out in the street
Tryin' to ease up on
some!

Need some Want some
Sure could use Some

Cried for some
Lied for some
Fell to my knees
And asked
GOD
To deliver me
Some

Still
Found none...

Lit candles for some
Burned incense for some
Got the
Holy Spirit
Sunday mornin'
Shoutin'
for
some

Closed my eyes
Heard your sighs
Woke up in the middle
of the night
Wailin' at the moon
Reachin'
for
some

I'm prayin' for some
Achin' for some
Your breath
That softsilky breeze
Caressin' my body
Makin' me
Moan
For
Some...

Magic

How can you be here
And there
At once?

I feel you
yet
I cannot see you.•.

I touch you
yet
. You are not present...

We speak
but
there are no words!!!

Must
be
Magic!

POETRY

Poetry is floetry
Questions...
Answers ...
Truth
Sometimes ....
A feeling
A dream
Once long sought
Nikki,
Langston,
e.e. too
The true rhyme in us
Has no hue!
Yeah!
Poetry!
That floetry
Indescribably
Deliciously
Thought provoking
In a tree
In the sky
Sun and moon
Sometimes a
Breathtaking swoon
Poetry ...
That Floetry!

BLACK AND TAN

The seeds from the
fruit
    of the
strange fruit tree
made their way
North
   and morphed
to a new variety
Bottom black
and a Paradise
Valley
back in the day
Same seed
New strand
this now known as
Black and Tan
In the clubs and the
Dance halls it rode
On the wind
The music and the
vibe
Drawing folks in
Rich, poor
black, white
The spirit of music
and love

It was an indigenous
Bottom Black
Culture
That carried the torch
Fueled by the likes
Of Howlin' Wolf
Dinah, Ray and of
course
The Count
Sassy Sarah too
The Black and Tans
Made the folks shout!
Club Plantation
Brown Bomber Shack
Let the people feel
The magic and the
light
Of the real deal
Della, Duke, Billy too
Practiced their craft
Among every hue
Sad to say
The glow of the night
Didn't cross into day
and become bright
light!

Lit up the night!
On Hastings
And St. Antoine
Northward bound

That made its way
to the Black and
Tans
From the seed
Of the strange fruit
The people that
mingled in the
night
Wouldn't be caught
together in
Broad daylight
The culture, the
music
And the divine vibe
Didn't cross into
day and spill
Outside
The Black and Tan
The people that
inhabited Paradise
Valley
And Bottom Black
Didn't experience
the
Glory of all of that

The day was clothed
in darkness and
despair
Vestiges of the DNA

Sad to say
Much mischief
Came to play
That shut the
Light shining bright
In the Black and Tans
In Bottom Black land
And a valley
Called Paradise
That lit up the night
Back in the day
When the music held
sway
And gathered clans
From all over the
land
In the Black and Tans
The mutated gene
Left the scene
That grew from the
seed
Of the
Southern fruit tree...

Inside
The Black and tan
Strange fruit...
Amazing, dismaying
Of what came to be
From the strange
fruit
That morphed
From the Southern
The Southern Fruit
Tree

1964

Freedom summer
Wasn't free
Bombings
Burnings
Lynching trees
Breaking chains
Spiritually ...
Terror rampant
Night
&
Day
Enlightened ones
Lead the Way ...

MEN

The men I know
Who have loved me in life
Are men who are men!
Willing to pay the price!
Men of color
Who love their mothers!
Men who strive
To keep family alive
Men who work Do their share
Providing for families
In their care!
Grandpa ... Daddy ...
Uncles ... Cousins ...
Nephews and brothers too
Are men who are doing
What Men are meant to do!
Caring!
Sharing!
Trusting God!
Men who love ...
Dance and sing!
Men unafraid of doin' their thing!
Men who grow strong
When life gives wrong!
Men who are examples
Of

The best there are to sample!
White chocolate
Dark chocolate
Sweet
Brown sugar too!
Long ... tall
Short ... round
Sweet/Bitter/
Sweet!
Fall down
Get UP!
Keep marchin' on!
Whole men
Broken men
Sad men
Confused men
Fallen men
Keep lookin UP
MEN!
Fall down ... Get UP!
Try again!
Get it right!
Stand fast in the night!
God gives you power
To shine your light!
Workin' ... hustlin'
Praying!
God
Blesses you for stayin'
MEN!

FREEDOM TIME

Once upon a time
The life of a black person
Did not seem worth a dime!

This mostly due
To the abuse and indignity
We have suffered through!

Bull Connor, George Wallace and the Klu Klux Klan
Wanted us to believe we were less than human!
Three fifths of a man
The Constitution once said
Trying to keep us all from moving ahead.

Quietly desperate
We went on to show
All those folks
It is just not so!

They found out
As time moved on
Indignity heaped on us
Eventually
Comes home!

Check it out
You will see
When cut with a knife
We all will bleed!

So, this is what I say to you:
Give everyone their just due!
'Cause sooner or later we will pay
When called to face our Judgement Day!

Learn the history!
Learn it fast!
OR
We are doomed
To repeat the past!

KIN

I am your sister
But you call me queer!
I am your sister
God put me here

He is your brother
Sent from Above!
Yet you maim and murder
Because of who he loves!

I am your sister
Filled with precious gifts!
I am your sister
Don't do me like this!

He is your brother
A man just like you!
He is your brother
Give him his due!

I want to know
What gives you the right?
To try to bring darkness
Where God put light!

You can't win
Don't you know?
'Cause fortunately it ain't you
Who runs the show!

We are your family
God is just!
We are your family
Love made us!

White Privilege

When you stand on your whiteness
And that's your major claim
You bring
Shame and derision to
God's holy name!
God is the author of
All that is
Beginning,
Middle and end
God created
This beautiful black skin
Red, brown, yellow too
Who are you
To demean,
Cheat and steal
Just so you
In your white skin
Can have your will
Greed, rape, murder
Enslavement
Is the poison you brew
Your whiteness becomes darkness'

Hate and despair
Sucking all the goodness
Out of
God's air!
God made this world
And all it holds!
Don't let your white skin
Kill your soul!
Drowned in a
lifeless
Godless hole!
White privilege!

THE MOVEMENT

The Movement
from whispering
pitter patter
to
deafening roar
Sacred hymns
providing beat
over
dark, blood stained
roads and streets
The Movement
Let the word go forth
soaked in love
Marching orders
from Above
The Movement
In the moment
From whispering pitter patter
to resounding roar
hate and judgment
Live here no more
The Movement
the beat
pitter patter million feet
The Movement
countless acts
of
Courage and strength

Fostering hope
Was not a joke!
The Movement
Continues to call
The Movement
forward
to
Abundance for All!
I don't know about you
I know about me
I need the you,
The us, the we
I need
The Movement!

Tower of Ivory
The Marygrove College Legacy

Who knew?
Can you believe it today?
The seeds of a dream
Bearing fruit
Today!

A dream remembered
Hope fulfilled
Tens of thousands
Lifted up a hill!

Buddings from this seed
Flower today:
Education, love, justice
Equality
For those in need!

A Tower of Ivory
Swathed
In a love
So bold!

A beloved dream
Of a sister of Soul
To deliver a gift
The Creator upholds!

Leading Sisters,
Servants, Immaculate Heart of Mary
With Theresa Maxis,
Blazing the way
They fed
And nurtured
A dream:
Competence,
Commitment,
Compassion
For all!
A way to overcome
What makes us small!

Intellectually, socially
That's for sure
Each class at Marygrove
Helped open a door!

From its beginnings
As one gender
To its diversity now
The Tower of Ivory
Still
Issues a call!

As we move forward
To a bright new day
The values we cherish
Uphold and sustain
Are borne
In new generations

Tower of Ivory
Aflame!

Looking forward
The legacy we cherish
Remains ablaze!

Competence
Commitment
Compassion
Have evolved to new heights!

Filled with holy boldness
We answer the call
That the21st century
Issues to all!

A legacy reimagined
Hopes renewed
Carry forward
The original call!

Human dignity
Community
Lead the list
As the Conservancy
Prepares
To continue uplift!

Social Justice
Care for the Earth
Diversity

Innovation
And unfettered
Imagination
Summon a new high
As we reach
For the sky!

The legacy is nurtured
In thought and deed
Living on in future generations
That have yet to breathe!

Tower of Ivory
Blazing bright!
Continuing a legacy
Of
Incomparable might!

JUDGE DAMON J. KEITH
IN MEMORY

A proverbial fist in a velvet glove
Of judicial fierceness
The Honorable Damon J. Keith
Humility, style, grace and flair
A conductor on a train
In rarefied air!
Scholarly, intellectually
Without compare
Damon J. Keith authored decisions
That helped take us there!
To justice, equality
Busing in Pontiac, police abuse
Discrimination lawsuits
He rendered decisions that removed any doubt
Of what justice and equality are all about
Helped level the field
With no ball, no bat
But with brains
and savvy under his hat!
In face of danger, murder, and mayhem
There was no fear that could delay him!
Dispensing a justice grounded in scholarship
and fact
Inspired in mind by the Divine!

We honor Judge Keith
For that divine, legal mind
His uncommon grace
And his unflinching commitment
To the least of us
In the running of his race!
Now he stands with the Ancestors
On a different plane
As a Spirit Guide
Helping justice be obtained!

Viola Gregg Liuzzo

In Memory

"Behold, Cometh a Dreamer, let us slay her"

She left her home
To help humankind
Become more kind
and
they killed her
said she asked for it
with a black man after dark
she made an easy mark
while helping humankind
become more kind
Selma, Alabama
In 1965
Dangerous to strive
To live a dream
I remember her name:
Viola Gregg Liuzzo
She left her home
Her babies
All she had known
To help humankind
Become more kind
and
they killed her

the KKK had their way
and killed her
remember her name
light a flame
help humankind
become more kind
like
Viola Gregg Liuzzo

Whitney Elizabeth Houston
In Memory

"We heard the testimony.
  We saw the evidence

It was a crime of passion
In every sense ..."
She sentenced us to be
Her lover for life
Sentenced by the notes
The pitch
The emotion

Snapshots in slow motion
Despite
drama
ish
Mucked up
Kinda sish
She convicted us
With a note
Anointed
Divinely ordained
Whitney Elizabeth
Sophisticated
Classy
Grown azz sassy!
Broken
Flawed
Vessel

Miracle
Who gives
'GOOD LOVE!'
We heard the testimony
We saw the evidence
Death don't win
'Cause love don't end
A miracle of love
Sent from above
Human .. Broken
Who will always love us with a note
'Cause
She was
Anointed
divinely ordained

We heard the testimony
We saw the evidence

Rev. Fred Shuttlesworth

In Memory

He said:
"I was born for this
time..."
Trials
Tribulations
Confrontation
Life on line
Bold, engaging teacher
A Shepherd
Born to lead
For this time
Bombings, beatings
Never ending threats
Hope in the Lord
Strength begets
Holy boldness dreams
For this time...

Daddy...
Protector, husband,
brotherman. Friend
Life on line
For this time...
Warrior, soldier
Light of God Beholder

Fiery
Fearless
Fred
Born for this time
Reverend Fred
Preacher
One sharp dressing
Regal Man
For this time
Life on line
Beat,
Head bowed
In prayer
Not defeat
For this time
Reverend Fred
Shuttlesworth
Gave us:
God's money worth
Spirit Bright
Shine
Not just for this time
But
All time!

Evelyne Bryant Deering ~ Mama

In Memory - January 1, 1929 - April 24, 2020

Mama dearest
Sister nearest
Intellectual fierceness
Despite
This Bitter Earth
and the days when
she drowned
in her own tears
and carried on
like mamas do
Makin somethin'
From nothin'
A black mama stew!
When God sent the man
with
'A Sunday Kind of Love'
It was
'Magic"
through
'September in the Rain'
Her love remained
Steadfast ...
Yeah,
Evelyne
Opening arms
Welcomed in
Family and friends

All the while
Firm, steady and able
Holding on
To God's
Unchanging hand!
Telling that hardhead man
'Try a Little Tenderness...'
'cause she loved him
'For Sentimental Reasons'
Bar-b-que goat, hoghead cheese,
Crowder peas
Throw in a little okra too
Seasoned to perfection
With a heart full of love!
Through Mabel Black Label
And that Dewar's White Label
Don't forget the milk
That went with it too!
Evelyne, mama
She's helped me laugh, dance, sing and grow
I want you to know that
She's my shero and so much good I've grown to be
Forever and always
The wind beneath my wings!

Author

Valerie Elaine Deering is an accomplished written and spoken word artist whose work centers around life, love and social justice.

Exposed to the work of e.e. cummings in elementary school, Valerie began a lifelong affair with the rhythm and rhyme of poetry, along with its ability to spark action, provoke thought and soothe the spirit.

A former educator, Valerie recognized the power of poetry in the classroom as a tool to convey concepts, ideas and facts through the rhythm, rhyme and imagery of the poetic word and often used poetry to achieve required goals and benchmarks.

Known best as The Nappy Headed Poet, Valerie has performed her work in churches, schools and spoken word venues in Detroit and Chicago. Additionally, Valerie was the featured poet for the Marygrove College Legacy event and the grand reopening of the Marygrove College Internet Archive Library.

A native Detroiter and graduate of Cass Tech High School, Valerie holds a B.A. degree in Political Science from Marygrove College; Detroit, Michigan and a M.S. in Early Childhood Education from Dominican University; River Forest, Illinois.

Contact Valerie for spoken word, to purchase books, to discuss her poetry, or book club events via:

Email: ValerieDeering20@gmail.com
Website: www.nappyheadedpoet.me
Facebook: nappyheadedpoet
Twitter: @nappyheadedpoet

CPSIA information can be obtained
at www.ICGtesting.com
Printed in the USA
LVHW051236010421
683211LV00004B/682